NO HANDS ALLOWED
A Robbie Reader

Ronaldinho

Rebecca Thatcher Murcia

Mitchell Lane
PUBLISHERS

P.O. Box 196
Hockessin, Delaware 19707
Visit us on the web: www.mitchelllane.com
Comments? email us: mitchelllane@mitchelllane.com

Printing   1   2   3   4   5   6   7   8

A Robbie Reader
No Hands Allowed

Abby Wambach	Brandi Chastain	Brian McBride
DaMarcus Beasley	David Beckham	Freddy Adu
Jay-Jay Okocha	Josh Wolff	Landon Donovan
Michael Owen	**Ronaldinho**	Ronaldo

Library of Congress Cataloging-in-Publication Data
Murcia, Rebecca Thatcher, 1962–
  Ronaldinho / by Rebecca Thatcher Murcia.
     p. cm. – (A Robbie reader. No hands allowed)
  Includes bibliographical references and index.
  ISBN 978-1-58415-600-0 (lib. bdg.)
  1. Ronaldinho, 1980– – Juvenile literature. 2. Soccer players–Brazil–Biography–
Juvenile literature. I. Title.
  GV942.7.R66M87 2008
  796.334092–dc22
  [B]
                                                                                    2007023486

ABOUT THE AUTHOR: Rebecca Thatcher Murcia grew up in Garrison, New York, and graduated from the University of Massachusetts at Amherst. She was a daily newspaper reporter–mostly in Texas–for 14 years. She is a soccer coach and player in Akron, Pennsylvania, where she lives with her two sons. She is the author of other soccer biographies for Mitchell Lane Publishers, including *Freddy Adu, David Beckham,* and *Landon Donovan.*

PHOTO CREDITS: Cover–Lars Baron/Bongarts/Getty Images; pp. 1, 3–Luis Bagu/Getty Images; pp. 14, 22–Friedemann Vogel/Bongarts/Getty Images; pp. 4, 6–Denis Doyle/ Getty Images; pp. 8, 10, 16–Jefferson Bernardes/Getty Images; p. 12–Andreas Rentz/ Bongarts/Getty Images; pp. 18, 21, 26–Lluis Gene/ AFP/Getty Images; p. 24–Cesar Rangel/AFP/Getty Images

ACKNOWLEDGMENTS: The following story has been thoroughly researched and to the best of our knowledge represents a true story. While every possible effort has been made to ensure accuracy, the publisher will not assume liability for damages caused by inaccuracies in the data. This story has not been authorized or endorsed by Ronaldinho.

TABLE OF CONTENTS

Ronaldinho is best known as a playmaker, a player who can set up creative passes for his teammates. He admires the American basketball player Michael Jordan, and imitates Jordan's famous no-look pass. But in his famous performance against Real Madrid, he twice dribbled past defenders and scored goals by himself.

Making Soccer History

Nothing like it had happened in Madrid's historic Bernabeu stadium in twenty-two years. Fans in general usually hold back their cheers for opposing players, even if they do something amazing. But on November 19, 2005, most of the 75,000 Real Madrid fans packing the huge stadium in Spain stood and cheered for Ronaldinho. The brilliant Brazilian midfielder for Real Madrid's rival, Barcelona, had just scored his second goal of the game, giving Barcelona a highly unusual 3-0 victory in an away game against Real Madrid.

Real Madrid was one of the richest clubs in Europe at the time. It had just spent millions of dollars to acquire David Beckham from Manchester United, and had a **roster** that was

Ronaldinho's skills often prompt defenders to make desperate attempts to take the ball away from him. In the November 19, 2005, game against Real Madrid, Sergio Ramos tried to stop Ronaldinho with a slide tackle, but Ronaldinho kept the ball and kept going.

packed with stars like the French player Zinedine Zidane and the Brazilians Ronaldo and Roberto Carlos.

That day in 2005, however, Ronaldinho and his teammates made Real Madrid look like a second-rate team. Ronaldinho was faking out Real Madrid with his dazzling moves and his pinpoint passes. First, Samuel Eto'o scored

15 minutes into the game. Then, in the second half, Ronaldinho received the ball near the midfield, **dribbled** effortlessly past two defenders, and fired a shot past Real Madrid's goalkeeper, Iker Casillas. With about 12 minutes left in the game, Ronaldinho again received the ball near the midfield, and again raced down the field and hammered the ball past Casillas.

"Incredible! Again! Ronaldinho!" the television announcer shouted in excitement. "Real Madrid does not have an answer for Ronaldinho!"

Gradually, the Real Madrid fans rose to their feet, clapping. They had not so honored an opposing player since they gave the Argentinean great Diego Maradona a standing **ovation** (oh-VAY-shun) in 1983.

"It was a perfect game," Ronaldinho told reporters after the game. "I will never forget this because it is very rare for any soccer player to be applauded in this way by the opposition fans."

Ronaldinho's family is very important to him. After he scores a goal, Ronaldinho looks up to heaven to thank his father, who died when he was eight years old. He is not embarrassed to be photographed kissing his mother.

Soccer and Sorrow

Ronaldinho was born on March 21, 1980. His full name is Ronaldo de Assis Moreira. His family lived in a poor neighborhood of Porto Alegre, a city in the south of Brazil. Ronaldinho has an older sister, Deisi, and an older brother, Roberto. Their father, Joao de Assis Moreira, was a welder, a night watchman for the popular local soccer club Gremio, and an **amateur** soccer player. Their mother, Miguelina de Assis Moreira, took care of the children and sold cosmetics door to door.

Ronaldinho started playing lots of soccer when he was five. He would play with the neighborhood children on a little field near his house. His father and his brother, Roberto, worked with him at their house to teach him

Ronaldinho's sister, Deisi (left), is his press coordinator. His brother (second from left) is his agent. Experts are often surprised that although Ronaldinho earns millions of dollars a year, he tries to keep his household operation fairly simple, just hiring a few family members to handle his business.

skills, but mostly Ronaldinho taught himself. He would play for hours with the ball, teaching himself to **juggle** it in the air with not only his feet, but also his knees, his head, and his chest. He also taught himself to dribble with speed and control. He watched **professional** players trick defenders with fakes and dribbling moves, and taught himself the same moves. Then he invented his own tricks. Sometimes his father

would see Ronaldinho dribbling too much in a game and would insist that he play with only two touches. "This took all the fun out of it for me and, at that age, made me very angry," Ronaldinho said later. "I cried. I didn't understand. But now I understand what he wanted."

Ronaldinho started going to soccer classes with the Gremio Soccer Club, where Roberto was developing into one of Brazil's best young players. The owners of the Gremio soccer club wanted to make sure Roberto stayed on their team, so they bought his family a large two-story house with a swimming pool. It seemed as though soccer had been a blessing for the family. But tragedy struck. On the day the family was planning to celebrate Roberto's eighteenth birthday and the parents' nineteenth wedding anniversary,

Ronaldinho thinks it is a great honor to wear his country's national team jersey. He always tries to do his best when playing for Brazil. Some observers, however, think he wears himself out playing for Barcelona and thus lacks energy for his national team games.

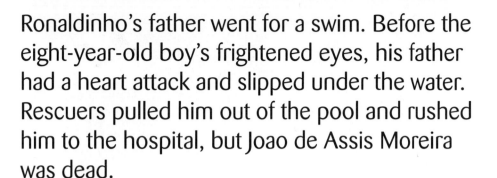

Ronaldinho's father went for a swim. Before the eight-year-old boy's frightened eyes, his father had a heart attack and slipped under the water. Rescuers pulled him out of the pool and rushed him to the hospital, but Joao de Assis Moreira was dead.

The death affected Ronaldinho, remembered Ronaldo Simonatto dos Santos, a neighbor whose children played with Ronaldinho. "He was timid, shy, like a scared little boy," said dos Santos, who would become like a substitute father. "He had a frightened look."

But Ronaldinho kept playing and getting better and better. He played a lot of futsal (*futebol de salão*), a particular kind of soccer that is very common in Latin America. It is usually played on an outdoor or indoor basketball court with a small, heavy, ball that doesn't bounce very much. Ronaldinho played on a **championship** Under-10 futsal team. He also played on a championship beach soccer team.

Ronaldinho is best known for his foot skills. In fact, he is also incredible with his thighs, head, and back. He doesn't just relax between games; he is always practicing and trying to improve.

An Incredible Youth Player

Brazil has won more **World Cups** than any other country, but until Ronaldinho and his fellow youth players came along in 1997, the awe-inspiring soccer nation had never won an Under-17 World Championship.

That year, Ronaldinho helped Brazil win the Under-17 World Cup in Egypt. He scored only two goals, but his grace and skill were apparent on the field. The next year, he was named to Gremio's senior team. The crowds loved his footwork and the joyful way in which he played.

In 1999, Gremio was playing its long-time rival, Internacional, for the state championship. Ronaldinho won the ball a few yards from Internacional's 18-yard box. He passed the ball

When people see Ronaldinho's joy and grace on the soccer field, they often liken him to a dancer. Indeed, Ronaldinho loves music. He likes to dance, sing, and play the drums.

to a teammate, who knocked it back to him in the air. In classic Ronaldinho fashion, he controlled the ball down to his chest at full speed, and then shot hard and low past the Internacional goalkeeper. It was the winning goal of the state championships.

In 1999, Ronaldinho also played for the senior Brazil team for the first time. He scored a beautiful goal against Venezuela in the America's Cup.

European clubs noticed Ronaldinho and began approaching his brother Roberto, who was acting as his agent. Ronaldinho signed a **contract** with Paris Saint-Germain, a French club. His move provoked a legal controversy because his contract with Gremio had not ended. FIFA, the international football federation, took charge of the matter and ordered Gremio to let Ronaldinho go. It forced Paris Saint-Germain to pay almost $6 million to Gremio for the rights to Ronaldinho.

Ironically, after fighting so hard to go to Europe, Ronaldinho did not appear to play his best at Paris Saint-Germain. There were moments when his brilliance shone through, but he did not get along well with the club's coach. He was also accused of spending too much time in Paris nightclubs and not enough time at practice.

Despite his rough time with the French club, he was still called up to play for Brazil in the 2002 World Cup. His chance to shine on the world stage approached.

Ronaldinho came into his own at Barcelona, where he earned the respect of his coaches, teammates, and fans with his skill, hard work, and generosity. At Barcelona, Ronaldinho teamed up well with Samuel Eto'o of Cameroon and Lionel Messi, the young Argentinean star.

World Cup Champions

The Brazilian national team arrived at the 2002 World Cup with lowered expectations. Their leading scorer, Ronaldo, had not been playing very well, and the team had not impressed fans in qualifying matches. But once the tournament began, the Brazilians, Ronaldinho included, began to show their top form. They cruised through their group, beating Turkey, Costa Rica, and China, and then defeating Belgium 2-0 in the first elimination round.

In the quarterfinals against England, Brazil got behind early after Michael Owen scored. Right before the first half ended, Ronaldinho won the ball near the midfield and darted toward the English goal with the ball at his feet.

An English defender approached, planning to steal the ball from Ronaldinho. Ronaldinho did a **scissor fake** that left the English player so confused, he fell down. As more defenders closed in on Ronaldinho, he rolled the ball perfectly to Rivaldo's feet on his right. Rivaldo scored. Brazil had tied the game 1-1.

Just a few minutes into the second half, Brazil was awarded a **free kick** about 40 yards from England's goal, on Brazil's right side. Ronaldinho ran to take the kick. The spot was so far away, players expected him to kick the ball in the air to the space in front of England's goal, with the hope that somebody could score from there. But Ronaldinho noticed that the English keeper, David Seaman, had come off the line in front of the goal, and he decided to shoot. The ball went up into a fairly high arc and then dropped right inside the upper left corner of the English goal, leaving Seaman backpedaling furiously but hopelessly. It was another incredible play by Ronaldinho.

In a much-disputed call, Ronaldinho was shown a **red card** after he fouled an English

Ronaldinho Gaucho, whose nickname "Gaucho" is a common term for people from Rio Grande do Sul in the south of Brazil, holds his 2006 FIFPro World Player of the Year award and his FIFPro World XI team trophies. FIFPro is the international organization of professional soccer players.

player. He was thrown out of the game against England with just a few minutes left. He had to sit out the semifinal against Turkey. But he was back on the field and played well in the final against Germany, which Brazil won 2-0 to claim the World Cup championship.

"When I was growing up, I never could have imagined that I would be at a World Cup, let alone win one," Ronaldinho said.

Ronaldinho's Barcelona team had to play Germany's Werder Bremen twice in Champions League in 2006. Ronaldinho performed one of his soccer magic tricks against Werder Bremen in the second game. He took a free kick about 20 yards from Werder Bremen's goal. Usually players try to serve free kicks around or over the wall formed by the opposing players, but Ronaldinho sent the ball under the wall to help his team win, 2-1.

CHAPTER FIVE

Success in Spain

After Ronaldinho's success in the World Cup, the best teams in the world were offering him millions of dollars for his soccer-playing talent. Ronaldinho chose to go to Barcelona, a romantic city on the Mediterranean coast of Spain. FC Barcelona had not won any major championships in recent years.

Barcelona won 17 straight games in Ronaldinho's first season, the championship of Spain in 2005, and the Champions League in 2006. Ronaldinho stood out, winning the award for the world's best soccer player in 2004 and 2005.

Also in 2005, he fathered a son, Joao, with a Brazilian girlfriend. The couple ended their relationship, but Ronaldinho supports the child

Barcelona lost against Liverpool in the Champions League in March 2007. Some reporters said Ronaldinho was not playing as well as in previous years. However, Barcelona was also playing without its star forward, Samuel Eto'o.

financially. He says that he loves children and hopes someday to marry and have a family. Meanwhile, he created a school, called the Ronaldinho Gaucho Institute, in his hometown in Brazil. The children there study arts, sports, and school subjects such as math and reading.

The highly praised Brazilian national team, the reigning world champions, were eliminated from the 2006 World Cup in Germany in the

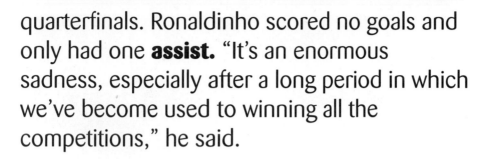

quarterfinals. Ronaldinho scored no goals and only had one **assist.** "It's an enormous sadness, especially after a long period in which we've become used to winning all the competitions," he said.

Ronaldinho also had his ups and downs on the field in 2007. Barcelona was eliminated early from the Champions League, and the team was not in first place in the Spanish League. But Ronaldinho's fame and fortune as a soccer player seemed to know no bounds. In spring of 2007, he took over David Beckham's spot as the highest paid player in the world, earning about $30 million per year. Nike launched an entire line of high-quality soccer

Ronaldinho's skills are recognized by players throughout the world. His teammate, defender Carlos Puyol, said, "If you don't foul him, it's impossible to stop him."

products based on the beloved Brazilian's belief in soccer, family, music, and his native country. Ronaldinho's star power continues to grow.

1980 Ronaldinho is born near Porto Alegre, Brazil, on March 21.

1989 His father, Joao de Assis Moreira, dies of a heart attack.

1997 Ronaldinho debuts for the Brazilian national team at the Under-17 World Cup in Egypt. (Players born after January 1, 1980, could play in the tournament.)

1999 Ronaldinho scores an amazing goal for Brazil's senior national team in a 7-0 rout of Venezuela for the America's Cup.

2001 Ronaldinho signs with Paris Saint-Germain.

2002 Ronaldinho plays on the victorious Brazilian World Cup team.

2003 Ronaldinho signs with FC Barcelona.

2004 He is voted FIFA's World Player of the Year.

2005 Ronaldinho's son, Joao, is born on February 25; Ronaldinho is again voted FIFA's World Player of the Year, and he earns a historic standing ovation in Madrid.

2006 Ronaldinho announces plans to open a school for poor children in his native Porto Alegre.

2007 *Forbes* names Ronaldinho the highest paid soccer player in the world.

amateur (AA-muh-chur)—a person who plays a sport for pleasure rather than for money.

assist—a pass that leads to a goal.

championship (CHAM-pee-un-ship)—a final game or series of games that decides which team is the winner of all the contenders.

contract (KON-trakt)—a written agreement between people or companies.

dribble—to use quick touches or light taps with the feet to move a soccer ball with control.

free kick—an unopposed kick given to a team when the referee decides someone on a team was fouled. Free kicks are also awarded when an opponent touches the ball with a hand or an arm.

juggle—in soccer, to keep a ball in the air by kicking it with the feet, or by hitting it with the thighs, chest, or head.

ovation (oh-VAY-shun)—expressing approval by clapping wildly.

professional (proh-FEH-shuh-nul)—someone who is paid to do a job.

red card—a signal given by a referee when a player commits an especially serious violation of the rules, such as violent play; the player is then removed from the game.

roster—the official list of the players on a team.

scissor fake—a move in which a player whips his feet around the ball in order to trick the opposing players.

World Cup—the international tournament for outdoor soccer.

Books

While there are no other books for young readers about Ronaldinho, you might enjoy these other soccer star biographies from Mitchell Lane Publishers:

Murcia, Thatcher Rebecca. *David Beckham.* Hockessin, Delaware: Mitchell Lane Publishers, 2005.

Murcia, Thatcher Rebecca. *Landon Donovan.* Hockessin, Delaware: Mitchell Lane Publishers, 2005.

Orr, Tamra. *Michael Owen.* Hockessin, Delaware: Mitchell Lane Publishers, 2006.

Orr, Tamra. *Ronaldo.* Hockessin, Delaware: Mitchell Lane Publishers, 2006.

Crisfield, Deborah. *The Everything Kids' Soccer Book: Rules, Techniques, and More About Your Favorite Sport!* Avon, Massachusetts.: Adams Media, 2002.

Web Addresses
ESPN Soccernet
http://soccernet.espn.go.com

FC Barcelona: Ronaldinho
http://www.fcbarcelona.com/web/english/futbol/
temporada_06-07/plantilla/jugadors/ronaldinho.html

FIFA: Brazil
http://www.fifa.com/associations/association=bra/
index.html

Major League Soccer
www.mlsnet.com

Sports Illustrated
http://sportsillustrated.cnn.com/

The United States National Soccer Players
www.ussoccerplayers.com

Works Consulted
Bell, Jack. "A Conversation with Ronaldinho." *The
    New York Times,* March 26, 2007. p. A01.
"Golden Boy." *The Daily Mail,* June 10, 2006, p. 110.
Kaufman, Michelle. "He's Got All the Right Moves;
    From the 'Elastico' to the 'Sombrero,'

Ronaldinho's Artistry is Mesmerizing Soccer Fans Worldwide." *The Miami Herald,* May 21, 2006, p. 1.

O'Connell, Michael. *Ronaldinho.* Great Britain: Artnik, 2007.

Ronaldinho: El Mejor Jugador del Mundo. (DVD) Gazeta Deportiva.

Settimi, Christina. "Kicking for Cash." *Forbes Magazine,* April 16, 2007. http://members.forbes.com/forbes/2007/0416/090.html

Smith, Alan. "Sitting at the Top of the World: Gifted, Humble Ronaldinho Is a True Credit to Soccer." *The Daily Telegraph,* May 17, 2006, p. B12.

Wahl, Grant. "Soccer's Sorcerer." *Sports Illustrated,* June 5, 2006, pp. 69–70.

Webster, Justin. "Homage from Catalonia." *Observer Sport Monthly,* June 5, 2005. http://football.guardian.co.uk/comment/story/0,,1499509,00.html